Salt Lake City

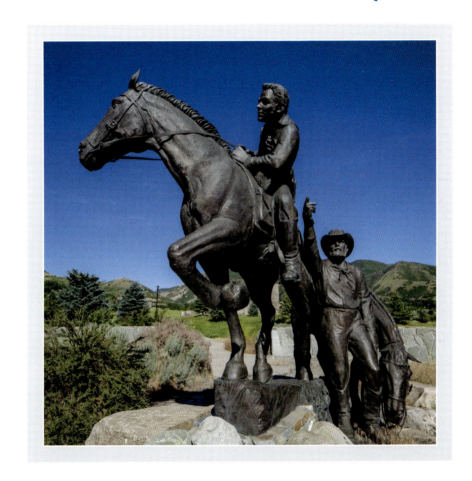

A PHOTOGRAPHIC PORTRAIT

Photography by Bill Crnkovich

Narrative by DeAnne Flynn

TWIN LIGHTS PUBLISHERS | ROCKPORT, MASSACHUSETTS

Copyright © 2013 by
Twin Lights Publishers, Inc.

All rights reserved. No part of this book may be reproduced in any form without written permission of the copyright owners. All images in this book have been reproduced with the knowledge and prior consent of the artists concerned and no responsibility is accepted by producer, publisher, or printer for any infringement of copyright or otherwise, arising from the contents of this publication. Every effort has been made to ensure that credits accurately comply with information supplied.

First published in the United States of America by:

Twin Lights Publishers, Inc.
51 Broadway
Rockport, Massachusetts 01966
Telephone: (978) 546-7398
http://www.twinlightspub.com

ISBN: 978-1-934907-22-1

10 9 8 7 6 5 4 3 2 1

(*opposite*)
State Capitol Dome Mural

(*frontispiece*)
Pony Express Monument

(*jacket front*)
Temple Square

Book design by:
SYP Design & Production, Inc.
www.sypdesign.com

Printed in China

SALT LAKE CITY. Nestled between prairie and ocean, this picturesque "crossroads of the west" welcomes the world to come and wholeheartedly experience her vast and varied landscapes, plentiful opportunities, and down-to-earth people.

Anciently, home to a mixture of Native American groups – including the Ute Tribe, from which Utah derives its name. Today, home to a mixture of people from many lands and cultures—Salt Lake City has long been a haven to those seeking sanctuary.

When Mormon pioneers wearily entered the desolate, uninhabited valley on July 24, 1847, searching for a refuge in which to practice their religion free from persecution, Church leader Brigham Young proclaimed, "This is the right place." So they immediately began planting crops, putting down roots, and planning their Zion.

Using engineering instruments brought from England, they established the easy-to-navigate street grid system Salt Lake City is well known for today. And soon the "Great Salt Lake City," named for the large salty lake that dominated the desert to the west, became a lush and thriving capital of industry.

Over the next several decades, thousands of European emigrants flocked to this rapidly growing valley, contributing their rich traditions, languages, and skills to advance the Great Salt Lake City into a flourishing cosmopolitan center.

And although the word "Great" had been dropped from the name Salt Lake City by May, 1869, this blossoming metropolis grew even more impressively as the masses traveled by rail to see the "City of the Saints" on the transcontinental railroad, which seamlessly connected East to West with the driving of a golden spike at Promontory Point.

Some people came to make their fortunes in mining—constructing large, gracious homes along South Temple, formerly Brigham Street. Others came, as did the first pioneers—to simply be free and begin anew.

By the early 1900s, Salt Lake City had begun to assume its present character—captivating, clean, and comfortable. And just one short century later, this renowned state capital grew large enough to host the extraordinary 2002 Olympic Winter Games, yet has remained cozy enough to offer horse-drawn carriage rides through the city center.

Indeed, the wise and careful planning of those early pioneers has positively paid off. Little did they know their beautiful Zion would one day be celebrated for Jell-O, fry sauce, and ice cream consumption, as well as for world-class opera, sports, and ballet.

Or that TRAX—the city's ever expanding, multi-million dollar light-rail system—would make traveling to school, to work, or to retail and recreational showpieces such a breeze. Industrious people, with big ideas, continue to be present-day pioneers as they strive to persistently improve this truly great Salt Lake City.

Indeed, scores still consider it to be "the right place."

Skyline

Cradled beneath the Wasatch Mountains, this city-extraordinaire melds tradition with fresh, innovative design. A vibrant metropolis continually being transformed by forward-thinkers, Salt Lake City is a leader in business, tourism, and research—devoted to excellence and a family-friendly way of life.

Salt Lake Tabernacle *(top)*

Remarkable acoustics, unobstructed views, and a superior organ were aspirations of LDS prophet, Brigham Young, when building the Salt Lake Tabernacle in 1867 where Latter-day Saints held General Conference for 132 years. Today, it hosts concerts and weekly broadcasts for the Mormon Tabernacle Choir.

Flowering Temple Square *(bottom)*

Drawing millions of visitors each year, Temple Square's ten-acre complex, owned by The Church of Jesus Christ of Latter-day Saints, is located in the heart of Salt Lake City. Temple Square visitors enjoy complimentary tours, performances, and plenty of photo ops, as well as relaxing garden strolls year round.

Temple Square *(opposite)*

Once Mormon pioneers entered the Salt Lake Valley in 1847, President Brigham Young declared, "Here we will build a temple to our God." The city block enclosing the chosen location became known as Temple Square; and in recent years, other church-owned facilities adjacent to the square have also been integrated.

Church Office Building *(opposite)*

Towering above Temple Square, the impressive 28-story Church Office Building houses support staff for the LDS Church's lay ministry worldwide. Offering stunning views from the Observation Deck on the 26th floor, this notable structure was once the tallest in the city. Complimentary tours are offered daily.

Brigham Young Monument *(above)*

Honoring pioneer-colonizer, Utah governor, and LDS Church president, Brigham Young, this 25-foot-tall bronze statue boldly stands at the intersection of Main Street and South Temple, paying homage to the visionary man who led the Mormon pioneers across the plains and into the barren Utah Territory in 1847.

Salt Lake Temple *(opposite)*

This exquisite edifice took 40 years to complete. Though it was the first temple pioneers began to construct in the Valley, it became the fourth when finally finished. With its distinctive spires and statue of the angel Moroni, this sacred sanctuary stands as an international symbol of the LDS Church.

Handcart Pioneer Monument *(above)*

Crafted by Norwegian-born sculptor, Torleif S. Knaphus, this revered statue captures the definitive Mormon pioneer spirit. A seven-foot-tall replica of a smaller work, this poignant monument immortalizes the nearly 3,000 pioneers who walked 1,350 miles to the Salt Lake Valley while pulling handcarts.

Temple Square *(pages 12 – 13)*

Millions of tiny lights glisten at dusk as Temple Square magically comes to life at Christmastime. Festive onlookers appear each evening to enjoy the month-long celebration, filled with activities, live concerts, and an impressive nativity scene depicting the birth of Jesus Christ, continuing through New Year's Eve.

City and County Building
(above, left, and opposite)

The prominent ten-acre site, known today as Washington Square, is home to Salt Lake City's distinguished City & County Building. Originally dedicated in 1894, this exquisite edifice once served as a hub for traveling American pioneers. It was later completely renovated, then rededicated in 1989.

State Capitol Building *(above and opposite)*

High on a majestic hill overlooking the city, this elegant architectural masterpiece captures history through beautiful artwork and educational exhibits. The Utah State Capitol Building, with its magnificent dome of Utah copper, was completed in 1916 using locally quarried granite. It was renovated from 2004-2008.

Mormon Battalion Monument *(above)*

Among several significant memorials honoring the courageous Mormon Battalion—the lone religious unit in American military history—only one stands on the Utah State Capitol grounds, culminating 22 years of intensive work by sculptor, Gilbert Riswold. The battalion served one year during the Mexican-American War.

Seagull Monument *(opposite)*

Created by sculptor, Mahonri M. Young, grandson of Brigham Young, the Seagull Monument is perfectly positioned in front of Assembly Hall on Temple Square. It commemorates what many in the LDS faith call "the miracle of the gulls," when cricket-eating seagulls miraculously saved the Mormon pioneer crops in 1848.

Council Hall

Ideally located just south of the State Capitol is Salt Lake City's historic Council Hall. Currently home to both the Utah Office of Tourism and the Utah Film Commission, this striking structure was originally called, "Salt Lake City Hall," but was relocated, renamed, and restored from 1961-1962.

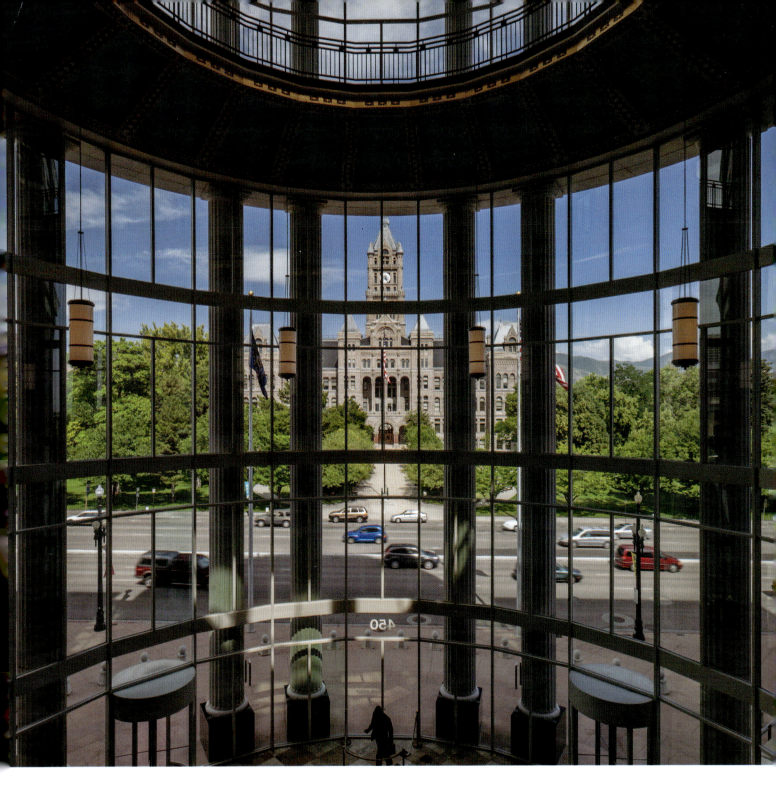

Scott M. Matheson Courthouse

Featuring a grand and glorious rotunda, the Scott M. Matheson Courthouse is home to the Utah Supreme Court, the Utah Court of Appeals, and the Salt Lake County Courts. Named for a former respected Utah governor, this dignified courthouse includes 37 courtrooms, in addition to the State Law Library.

Steiner American Building

In 1895, George A. Steiner began propelling the Steiner American Company into an internationally recognized icon in linen supply. In 1967, it became one of the first private companies to move its headquarters to South Temple and constructed a uniquely modern, award-winning building—still in use today.

Pioneer Memorial Museum

Visitors of all ages regularly walk back into history at the Pioneer Memorial Museum, also known as the Daughters of the Utah Pioneers Museum. Featuring collections of memorabilia from the earliest Utah pioneers, this ancient-treasure-keeper boasts the world's largest collection of artifacts on a specific subject.

Temple Square North Visitors' Center
(above and opposite)

Temple Square guests often stand beneath the star-studded dome of the North Visitors' Center rotunda, viewing a magnificent 11-foot-tall statue of The Christus, by Bertel Thorvaldsen. Although the original stands in the Church of Our Lady in Copenhagen, Denmark, this replica at the Temple Square North Visitors' Center is magnificent.

Salt Palace Convention Center *(opposite, top)*

In the heart of downtown Salt Lake City, the Salt Palace Convention Center hosts meetings, conferences, and gatherings of every size. With delicate snowflake chandeliers and musical wind chimes in its five-story main concourse, this is an architectural and modern art mecca.

James L. Sorenson Molecular Biotechnology Building *(opposite, bottom)*

Dedicated in 2012, the James L. Sorenson Molecular Biotechnology Building on the U of U campus has become a useful "bridge" by allowing passage through traditional boundaries, accelerating research in the fields of medicine, pharmacology, engineering, and computer and life science.

Grand America Hotel *(above)*

Luxurious and elegant, The Grand America shines as Salt Lake City's only AAA Five Diamond hotel. Built in the lavish style of Europe's finest hotels for the 2002 Olympic Winter Games, this extraordinary showpiece features beautifully landscaped gardens, finely appointed decor, and exceptional gourmet cuisine.

Family History Library *(above)*

The largest library of its kind in the world, the Family History Library was established in 1894 by the LDS Church to gather genealogical records and support citizens in their family history and genealogical research. Hosting approximately 1,500 visitors daily, it is open to the public free of charge.

The City Library *(opposite)*

Winner of Library Journal's "Library of the Year Award" in 2006, the remarkable City Library stands as a "dynamic civic resource—fostering creativity, encouraging the exchange of ideas, building the community, and enhancing the quality of life" for nearly 200,000 fortunate Salt Lake residents and their families.

Church History Library and Archives

Collections at this stunning archive chronicle The Church of Jesus Christ of Latter-day Saints from its beginning in 1830 to the present day. These impressive collections contain manuscripts, books, photographs, church records, oral histories, architectural drawings, pamphlets, newspapers, periodicals, maps, microforms, and audiovisual materials.

Church History Museum

The Church History Museum at Temple Square brings the compelling history of the LDS Church to life through exhibits and interactive programs. This premier museum collects and displays interesting LDS art and artifacts from around the world and offers complimentary tours for the entire family.

LDS Conference Center *(top)*

Likely the largest theater-style auditorium ever built, the LDS Conference Center is now the principal gathering place for The Church of Jesus Christ of Latter-day Saints. Finished in 2000, this 1.4 million-square-foot center seats 21,200 people in its main auditorium, providing unobstructed views for all.

Mormon Pioneer Memorial *(bottom)*

This downtown Salt Lake City memorial is dedicated to the more than 6,000 pioneers who died making the journey to Utah from all parts of the world between 1847 and 1869. It is the gravesite of Brigham Young, Mary Angell, Eliza R. Snow, and other early pioneers and Mormon leaders.

Assembly Hall *(opposite)*

One of the unforgettable buildings in Salt Lake City, Assembly Hall was completed in a Gothic style by 1882 using mostly granite discarded from the temple building process. Conveniently placed on the southwest corner of Temple Square, it has traditionally been used for musical performances and religious meetings.

First Presbyterian Church

On April 16, 1905, over one thousand Presbyterians gathered at their new sandstone church, marking the first service on C Street and South Temple. Designed by Utah architect, Walter E. Ware, this castle-style masterpiece features seven brilliant memorial stained-glass windows chronicling the life of Jesus Christ.

Empty Tomb

Just as the morning sun peeks over the mountains, the angel in this stunning stained-glass mural begins to illuminate Salt Lake's First Presbyterian Church. Depicting Christ's "Empty Tomb," this inspiring window was designed by R.T. Giles and Co. of Minneapolis, Minnesota just in time for Easter 1906.

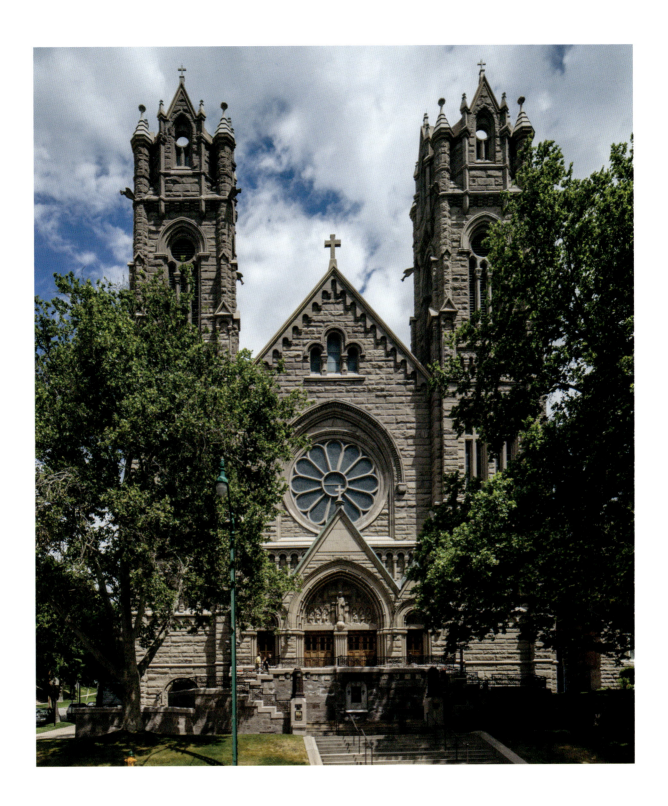

St. Mark's Episcopal Cathedral *(opposite)*

The third oldest Episcopal cathedral in the U.S., Saint Mark's Episcopal Cathedral, was designed in the neo-Gothic style by noted architect, Richard Upjohn. Consecrated in 1874, this cathedral is still being used for worship services, musical and civic events, and also for community outreach programs.

Cathedral of the Madeleine *(above)*

Utah's first grand cathedral was proudly dedicated in 1909 at 133 East South Temple. It was designed by prominent Utah architect, Carl M. Neuhausen, in a Romanesque style using round Roman arches and rough-cut stone. The exterior of the cathedral looks substantially the same today as it did in 1909.

Cathedral of the Madeleine Interior

Though this magnificent structure has undergone numerous renovations, the most extensive took place between 1991 and 1993 at a cost of $9.7 million, involving every aspect of the interior. This stunning edifice was formally rededicated in 1993 and is currently listed on the National Register of Historic Places.

Joseph Smith Memorial Building
(above and opposite)

Originally the grand Hotel Utah, dating back to 1909, this majestic 10-story Renaissance Revival style structure is still inspiring visitors with its ambiance and splendor. On the corner of Main and South Temple, it is now home to special events, superb restaurants, a state-of-the-art FamilySearch Library, and LDS offices.

Social Hall Heritage Museum *(bottom)*

The notable Social Hall Heritage Museum, located at 51 South State Street, is dedicated to the lighter side of pioneer life. Remains of the original Social Hall, where early residents enjoyed singing, dancing, and wholesome entertainment, were discovered in 1991 and preserved for public viewing everyday except Sunday.

Devereaux Mansion *(above)*

Salt Lake City's earliest mansion, the elegant Devereaux, remains an ideal setting for social gatherings. Original owner, William Jennings, furnished the rich interior with exceptional items collected while traveling. Portions of the house date back to 1855, only eight years after the Mormon pioneers entered the Valley.

Governor's Mansion *(opposite, top)*

Once host to President Roosevelt, U.S. Senator and "Silver King," Thomas Kearns, built this opulent mansion in 1902. Kearns' widow, Jennie, donated it to the state in 1937 and for 20 years Utah governors lived here while in office. In 1980, the Kearns Mansion once again became the Governor's residence.

Enos Wall Mansion *(opposite, bottom)*

A substantial 1881 home stood on this property when purchased by mining boss, Enos Wall, in 1905. Wall hired Richard K. A. Kletting, who later designed the Utah State Capitol, to enlarge this neoclassical manor. Later, it was home to the Salt Lake Jewish Center, then LDS Business College purchased it for community use.

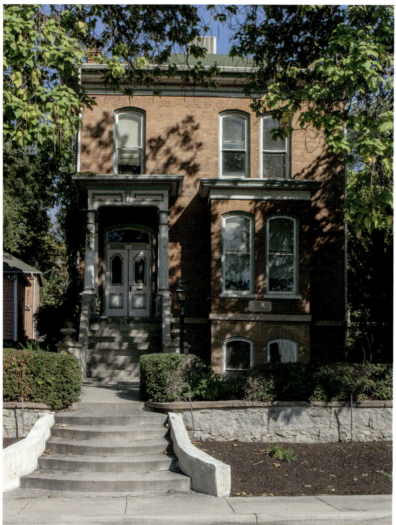

Marmalade District *(above and left)*

Settled in Salt Lake City's early days, the Marmalade Hill Historic District's streets were named after fruits that are typically found in marmalades and jams. Distinguished by mature landscaping and an impressive array of vintage homes, this section of Capitol Hill is perhaps Utah's best example of eclectic, well-preserved architecture.

McCune Mansion *(opposite)*

Early American railroad tycoon, Alfred W. McCune, and his wife, Elizabeth, built this mansion as a family home at a cost of $1,000,000.00 in 1901. The McCarthey Family purchased the mansion in 1999 and generously returned it to its original splendor. Today, it is home to events, meetings, and weddings.

Lion House

The Lion House was built in 1856 by Brigham Young for his family and remains largely vintage today, featuring antique furnishings, fixtures, and art. Known for exceptional catering, it's an ideal spot for special events, family gatherings, business meetings, parties, and weddings—combining hospitality with historic elegance.

Beehive House

Once home to LDS Church President and Utah Territory Governor, Brigham Young, the Beehive House stands one block east of the Salt Lake Temple. Past Church presidents Lorenzo Snow and Joseph F. Smith also lived, and both died, in the Beehive House. Complimentary 20-minute tours are available daily.

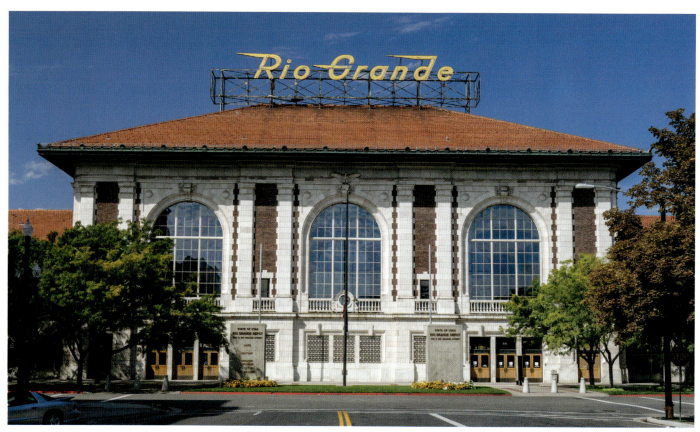

Denver and Rio Grande Depot *(opposite, top)*

The Denver and Rio Grande Depot opened in 1910, an impressive entrance for a city that had almost doubled in population during the previous decade. Both striking and spacious, this historic depot was purchased in 1977 by the state of Utah. Restored government offices now occupy this building.

Salt Lake Stock and Mining Exchange Building *(opposite, bottom)*

In an effort to make south downtown the "Wall Street of the West," Samuel Newhouse donated this site to the Salt Lake Mining and Stock Exchange in 1908. The street upon which it stood was named Exchange Place for its role in building a western financial hub.

Eagle Emporium Building *(above)*

Utah's first millionaire, William Jennings, constructed this building in 1864, now the oldest existing commercial structure downtown. Once home to the LDS Church-owned Zion's Cooperative Mercantile Institution (ZCMI), it later housed several businesses. The ornate clock is a treasured piece of 19th-century history.

Eagle Gate Monument *(opposite, top)*

Erected in 1859 at the entrance to Brigham Young's property leading to City Creek Canyon, the Eagle Gate Monument looms impressively overhead. Replacing the original wooden bird, the present bronze eagle majestically extends her wingspread 20 feet wide and weighs approximately 4,000 pounds.

Masonic Temple *(opposite, bottom)*

Since 1927, the Salt Lake Masonic Temple has served as the Masonic headquarters for Utah, and is a fine example of Egyptian Revival architecture. Located in the prestigious South Temple Historic District, this building has remained in continual use since its original construction and subsequent renovations.

Union Pacific Railroad Depot *(above)*

At an estimated cost of $450,000, the Union Pacific Railroad Depot was constructed in 1909. It was later restored as the grand entrance to The Gateway, a multi-use retail plaza. This mural by San Francisco artist, John McQuarrie, marks the arrival of Mormon pioneers into the Valley in 1847.

New York Hotel *(top)*

Salt Lake's Gastronomy Restaurant Group, Inc. owns several consistently "Top" rated eateries in the Salt Lake City area. Three of their nine superb restaurants are located in the historic 1906 New York Hotel: the New Yorker, the Market Street Oyster Bar, and the Market Street Grill. Each serves daily.

Market Street Grill *(bottom)*

Reminiscent of grills from the 1930s with long counters, bead board, and subway tile floors, the #1 Zagat-rated Market Street Grill is known for its variety of fresh seafood, flown in daily since 1980, in addition to succulent steaks, exceptional clam chowder, tasty salads, and fresh sourdough bread.

Squatters Brewery

Squatters is an innovative dining establishment featuring world-class beer, delicious food, and a welcoming atmosphere. Touting a long list of awards, Squatters Pub Brewery downtown, and at the Salt Lake International Airport, both offer excellent service while possessing the charm and ambiance of a local pub.

Olympic Snowflake Fountain *(top)*

Well positioned at The Gateway, a prime outdoor shopping, dining, entertainment, and residential center, the Olympic Fountain is difficult to resist on a hot summer day. Children love to play in this snowflake-shaped cascade, which features dancing jets of water synchronized to inspiring music every 30 minutes.

Olympic Legacy Plaza *(bottom)*

Near the Olympic Fountain at The Gateway is the Olympic Legacy Plaza, displaying wide granite panels etched with the names of financial donors, as well as more than 28,000 volunteers who generously and selflessly sacrificed their time to help the Salt Lake 2002 Olympic Winter Games become legendary.

Go for the Gold

Exhibited at The Gateway's Olympic Legacy Plaza, this striking bronze statue of an Olympic skier was donated by Robert L. Rice and Kenneth O. Melby. Go for the Gold was created by Jonathan Bronson for the 2002 Olympics and uniquely enhances this extraordinary retail, office, and residential hub.

Gallivan Center *(opposite)*

Also known as "Salt Lake's Living Room," the Galivan Center is home to a variety of events, concerts, festivals, receptions, meetings, and weddings, as well as a fun-filled ice-skating rink. Built for the 2002 Olympic Winter Games, this popular center is conveniently located downtown and is open year-round.

Capitol Theatre *(above)*

One of Salt Lake's most dearly loved buildings, the Capitol Theatre has been a landmark since 1913. Vaudevillians were king here for years, but in 1978 the theatre was renovated and reopened. This theatre is currently home of Ballet West, Utah Opera, Children's Dance Theatre, and Broadway Across America-Utah.

Independence Day *(pages 58–59)*

Excitement soars over Salt Lake City as Independence Day firework celebrations extend across the Valley. With roots tracing back to the mid-1800s, these high-spirited events draw hundreds of thousands of spectators each year, honoring the traditional American values of family, freedom, and love of country.

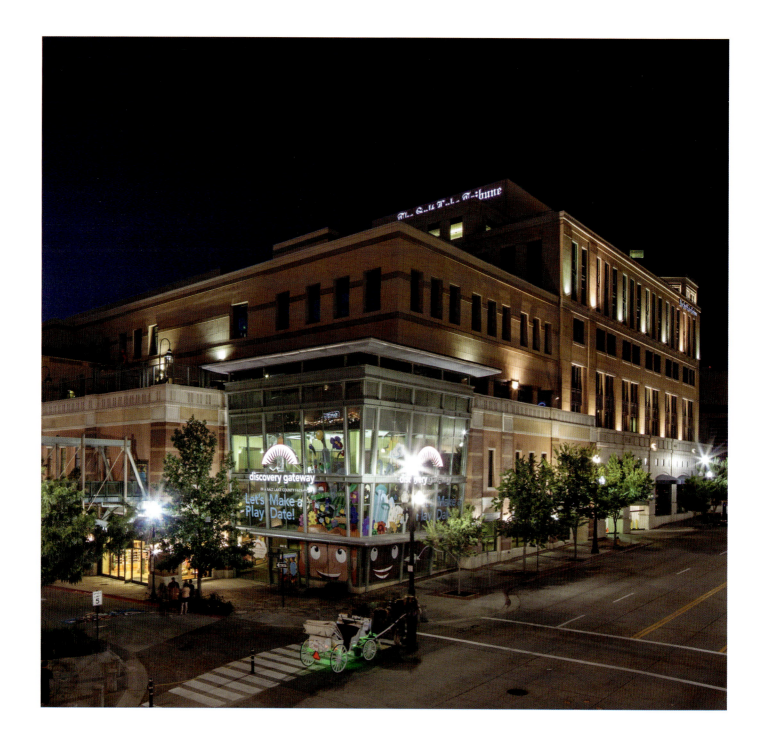

Discovery Gateway Children's Museum

Founded in 1978 by a group of parents, educators, and community leaders who believed children learn best by "doing," the Discovery Gateway Children's Museum offers a variety of learning experiences for the young and young-at-heart. With its new expansive location at The Gateway, there's now 60,000 square feet of fun.

Hands On Fun *(left and right)*

Inspiring, inviting, interactive, and interesting are the exhibits at this kid-friendly gathering place, where children can use their imaginations freely, as well as their hands and feet. Touching is not off limits here. In fact, this innovative learning center encourages tactile interaction and creative play with welcoming attractions like these.

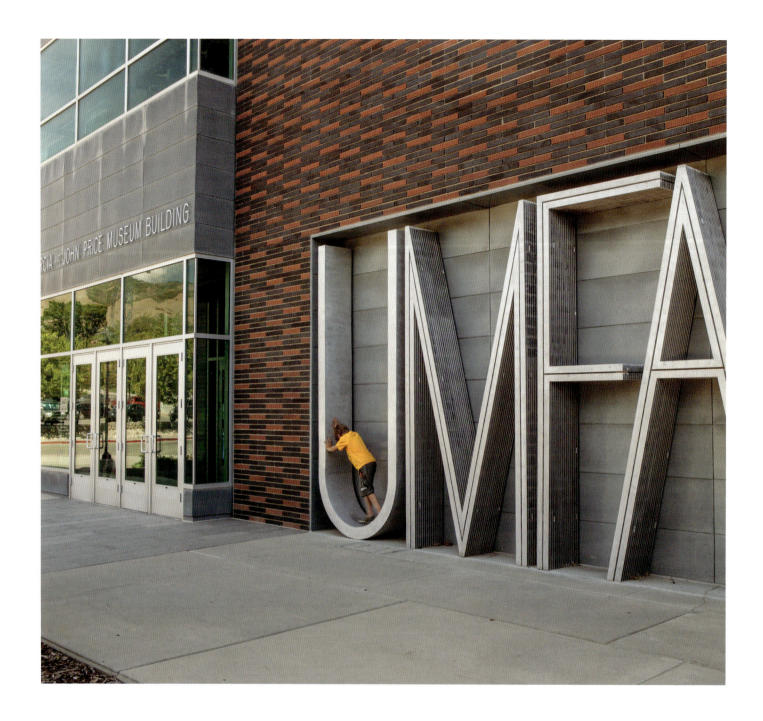

Utah Museum of Fine Arts

In the heart of the University of Utah campus stands a revered treasure-trove of fine collections. The Utah Museum of Fine Arts proudly displays continually rotating works of art in 20 handsome galleries. Both a university and a state-of-the-art showplace, it houses more than 17, 000 unique works.

The Leonardo

Unique, interactive exhibits lace The Leonardo where science, technology, art, and creativity connect. Located in downtown Salt Lake City, this contemporary museum offers educational programs, traveling exhibits, and classes in the former SLC Public Library, which has been serving the Wasatch Front for nearly 50 years.

Flying Objects

Feathers in the Wind, by sculptor, Greg Ragland, stands in front of Abravanel Hall at 123 West South Temple. This fabricated steel showpiece is part of "Flying Objects 3.0"—a series of artistic works fashioned by creative Park City-based Ragland, who received his MFA from the University of Utah.

Utah Museum of Contemporary Art

Heralded as both a creative pioneer and an artistic champion, The UMOCA exhibits progressive artwork by local, national, and international artists. This groundbreaking art abode is winner of the 2011 and 2012 "Utah's Best Museum" award, and is a four-time recipient of funding from the Andy Warhol Foundation.

Clark Planetarium

Replacing the Hansen Planetarium, this state-of-the-art science center opened at The Gateway in April 2003. The Clark Planetarium's theater is the first "pitless" digital dome planetarium in the nation, offering 205 seats, each with interactive controls. It also houses an IMAX theater and numerous interactive displays.

Maurice Abravanel Hall

Home of the renowned Utah Symphony and celebrated for its crystal clear acoustics, Abravanel Hall is both an architectural and artistic landmark. Originally "Symphony Hall" in 1979, the building underwent a major renovation. It was renamed in 1993 for Maurice Abravanel, a former conductor of the Utah Symphony.

City Creek Center *(above)*

Waterfalls, foliage-lined walkways, fountains, and streams grace this three-block shopper's paradise in the heart of downtown. Opening to the public with rave reviews in March 2012, this retail showpiece is one of the largest mixed-use downtown redevelopment projects in the nation. It also boasts a retractable roof.

Transcend Fountain *(opposite)*

The magnificent Transcend Fountain at the City Creek Center was designed by WET Designs, creators of the Bellagio fountains in Las Vegas. With choreographed lights, water, and fire on the half hour, this eye-catching fountain adds excitement and beauty to City Creek's 20 acre residential, shopping, and office complex.

Flutter Fountain

This awe-inspiring, mixed-use retail, residential, and recreational hub hosts more than 90 stores and restaurants, a gourmet grocer, and six acres of well-maintained green space. With splendid water features like the graceful Flutter Fountain, the City Creek Center attracts urban dwellers, shoppers, and business-people alike.

TRAX

In addition to keeping the properties surrounding Temple Square economically vibrant, the City Creek Center conveniently links two city blocks across Main Street with a covered pedestrian skyway. Serviced by the "City Center" TRAX light rail station, this area is also accessible by car and offers underground parking.

Pioneer Day Celebration *(top and bottom)*

Marking the arrival of Mormon Pioneers into the Salt Lake Valley on July 24, 1847, Utahns commemorate this official state holiday in grand style with a parade, a multi-day rodeo, and a variety of annual festivities. Similar to the 4th of July, government offices and many businesses close to celebrate.

Utah State Fair

Opening the first Thursday after Labor Day, this 11-day fair is overflowing with food, fun, exhibits, and prizes. From concerts and demolition derbies in the grandstands, to livestock and agriculture in the exhibit halls—there's something for everyone at this annual Utah State Fairpark event, which began in 1856.

Huntsman Cancer Institute

The only National Cancer Institute-designated center in the Intermountain West, the Huntsman Cancer Institute prides itself on providing the most current cancer screening, diagnostic, and treatment methods. Philanthropist Jon Huntsman, Sr. has donated over $250 million to this center that is located at the University of Utah.

University of Utah

This renowned, state-owned research institution offers more than 100 undergraduate and 90 graduate degree programs to nearly 30, 000 students each year. Among the finest publicly-funded universities, it features a nationally ranked law school, superior athletic programs, and hosts the only medical school in Utah.

Vietnam Veterans Memorial *(top)*

Located on the State Capitol grounds, the Vietnam Veterans Memorial honors the Utahns that unselfishly served the cause of freedom. This courageous soldier was sculpted by Mark Davenport, and the surrounding wall was created by Clyde "Ross" Morgan. It contains the names of 388 fallen Vietnam War soldiers.

Hoberman Arch *(bottom)*

Located at the south end of Rice-Eccles Stadium on the University of Utah campus is Olympic Cauldron Park. This plaza contains the 2002 Winter Olympic Visitors' Center, cauldron, and other memorabilia. The striking Hoberman Arch was originally a mechanical curtain for the Olympic Medal Plaza's stage.

Olympic Cauldron *(opposite)*

At a cost of $2 million, the 2002 Olympic Cauldron's icicle shape was inspired by the motto, "Light the Fire Within." Designed by WET Design and built by Arrow Dynamics, the cauldron was unveiled at Rice-Eccles Stadium in January 2002, and was later moved to the Olympic Cauldron Park.

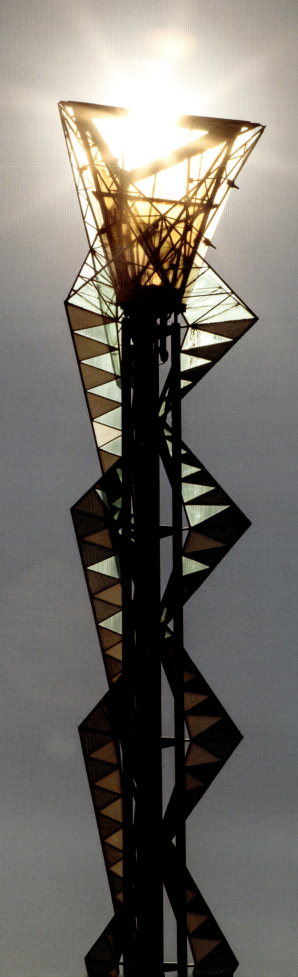

Natural History Museum of Utah *(top)*

Featuring hands-on, interactive exhibits for the entire family, vistors can get back to nature at the Natural History Museum of Utah. Located along the Bonneville Shoreline Trail, a popular location for hiking and mountain biking, it's an ideal destination for those interested in learning more about Utah's natural history.

Dinosaur Collection *(bottom)*

With impressive collections in Paleontology, Anthropology, Entomology, Vertebrate Zoology, Mineralogy, Botany, and Malacology (seashells), this innovative museum strives to "illuminate the natural world and the place of humans within it." Collections from the Cleveland-Lloyd Dinosaur Quarry are world famous.

Rio Tinto Center

Positioned prominently in the foothills above Salt Lake City, the Natural History Museum of Utah now thrives in its new home, the Rio Tinto Center. This extraordinary, copper-clad building rests on a series of terraces that follow the shape of the hillside and blend in with the natural environment.

Red Butte Garden *(top)*

Operated by the University of Utah in the foothills of the Wasatch Mountains, Red Butte Garden and Arboretum is a non-profit botanical and ecological center. This popular day and field trip destination is where an extensive variety of plants are cultivated for scientific, educational, and ornamental purposes.

Waterfall Garden *(bottom)*

When seeking a natural escape from the stress and cares of the world, Red Butte Garden is a perfect place to brighten up a morning or to spend a lazy afternoon. Open year-round to the public, admission is always free on Arbor Day, and special events abound near holidays.

Herb Garden *(above)*

This garden paradise features scenic walking paths, hiking trails, and landscaped grounds. Offering a variety of nature-related classes and events, Red Butte Garden hosts a series of summer concerts, as well as floral, sculpture, and other art exhibits in its Conservatory and Visitors' Center.

A Living Landscape *(pages 82–83)*

In an effort to "cultivate the human connection with the beauty of living landscapes," the U of U donated 100 acres at the mouth of Red Butte Canyon in 1983. Red Butte Garden has become the largest botanical garden in the Intermountain West, which tests, displays, and interprets regional horticulture.

Memory Grove Park

Dedicated in 1920, Memory Grove Park celebrates the lives of Utah veterans from World War I, World War II, and the Vietnam War. City Creek ripples through the lush park, and trails lead up into City Creek Canyon—a favorite for dog owners who come to take advantage of the scenic off-leash areas.

Meditation Chapel

In the foothills of the city, immediately east of Capitol Hill, stands beautiful Memory Grove Park. This revered, hidden oasis includes the Meditation Chapel, which was built in 1948 by Mr. and Mrs. Ross Beason as a memorial to their son and other Utahns who died in World War II.

Liberty Park

Salt Lake City's second-largest urban green-space, Liberty Park features 80 acres of grass and trees, a pond with two islands, playgrounds, a bowery, jogging paths, a bird refuge, a large greenhouse, sport courts, and more. During the summer months, paddleboats, recreational games, and picnics are common here.

Tracy Aviary *(above and right)*

Since 1938, Liberty Park has been harboring a hidden sanctuary, Tracy Aviary. Home to more than 400 birds, representing 135 species, this fascinating destination has a mission of "fostering concern for the natural world" and attracts birds from around the Valley to its numerous waterways, trees, and nesting grounds.

International Peace Gardens

Demonstrating that people from many lands can come together to promote peace and understanding, the International Peace Gardens were conceived in 1939 and dedicated in 1952. Twenty-six countries are represented by unique, culturally appealing gardens on the banks of the Jordan River near Salt Lake City.

Swiss Matterhorn Monument

In an effort to beautify and improve the Swiss plot at the International Peace Gardens, this fifty-foot replica of Switzerland's most famous mountain was completed in 1963. Native plants and mature trees, a Swiss chalet with a granary, and a pond with a rustic bridge also adorn this lovely garden.

Plum Pavilion *(above)*

Since 1953, the Plum Pavilion has been a prominent feature of the Chinese plot at the International Peace Gardens. The marble lions placed at the entrance were gifts from the Chinese Cultural Center in 1979. They symbolize friendship and understanding between the Republic of China and Salt Lake City.

Our Hope for the Children *(opposite)*

Gifted sculptor, Avard Fairbanks, added this striking monument to Salt Lake City's International Peace Gardens in 1976. The monument is comprised of two Fairbanks sculptures: Our Hope for the Children and Peace on Earth. These cast stone statues represent the dawn of a new era and greatly enhance the gardens.

Trolley Square *(above and opposite)*

Once a barn for storing electric trolleys when the city was serviced by a rail streetcar system, this mission style complex became an upscale shopping center during the 1970's. Presently, Trolley Square hosts some of the nation's premiere retailers and restaurants, in addition to a comedy club and a fitness facility.

This is the Place Heritage Park

This fun-filled Visitor Center is a sugar mill replica, originally built in 1853 for the Salt Lake community called Sugar House. Today, it houses a gift shop, the Mormon Battalion Museum, and the Stoddard Art Gallery. Guests watch movies here, as well as shop for nostalgic candy and pioneer memorabilia.

This is the Place Monument

One hundred years after Mormon pioneers entered the Valley, this monument was erected near Emigration Canyon to honor them. Sculpted between 1939 and 1947 by Mahonri M. Young, grandson of Brigham Young, these impressive statues were dedicated on July 24, 1947 by LDS Church President, George Albert Smith.

Gristmill

Originally built in Manti, Utah in 1854, this gristmill replica was constructed in 1997 at This is the Place Heritage Park. The gristmill, where grain was ground into flour, was an essential part of early pioneer settlements. This limestone gristmill contained two sets of millstones, each were powered by a waterwheel.

This is the Place Heritage Park *(top and pages 98 – 99)*

In the foothills above Salt Lake City, visitors discover the rugged, captivating past by exploring the buildings, homes, and businesses brought skillfully back to life at this recreated pioneer village. Weddings, tours, and community events are commonplace here, as are youth service programs.

Living History *(bottom)*

Touted as "Utah's premier living history attraction," Heritage Park's guests step back in time and experience the Old West the way it once was. Dressed in period attire, pioneer recruits teach practical lessons, forgotten skills, and the many bygone secrets settlers used to make life simpler and more productive.

97

Fort Douglas Military Museum
(above and left)

Formerly a 19th-century barracks, built of Red Butte sandstone on the University of Utah campus, the Fort Douglas Military Museum was officially opened in 1976 to remember and honor the men and women who have "served their country in uniform, protecting our cherished way of life with their sacrifices."

Deuel Pioneer Log Cabin

One of the oldest homes in Salt Lake City, this authentic log cabin offers fascinating insight into early pioneer life. Built in 1847 by the William Henry Deuel family, it is now fully restored, furnished with pioneer artifacts, and is open to the public on West Temple, across from Temple Square.

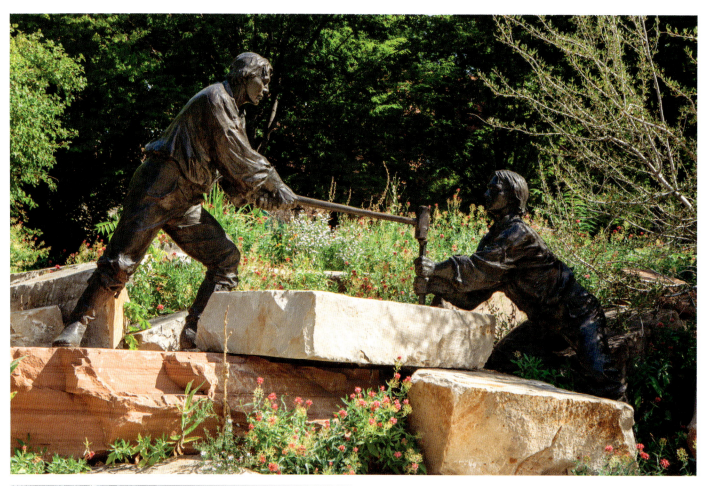

Brigham Young Historic Park
(above and left)

Just east of Temple Square stands a lush green oasis, featuring a variety of beautiful statues honoring courageous pioneers and their leaders. These memorials include likenesses of Latter-day Saint prophets, such as Joseph Smith and Brigham Young, who inspired the early Saints, and still remain important LDS figures today.

Waterwheel *(opposite)*

This historic park, created to honor the LDS prophet leader, Brigham Young, has an authentic pioneer flavor. Featuring a massive waterwheel that churns City Creek along its path, summer months are especially popular here since concerts and Wednesday evening talks are free of charge to the public.

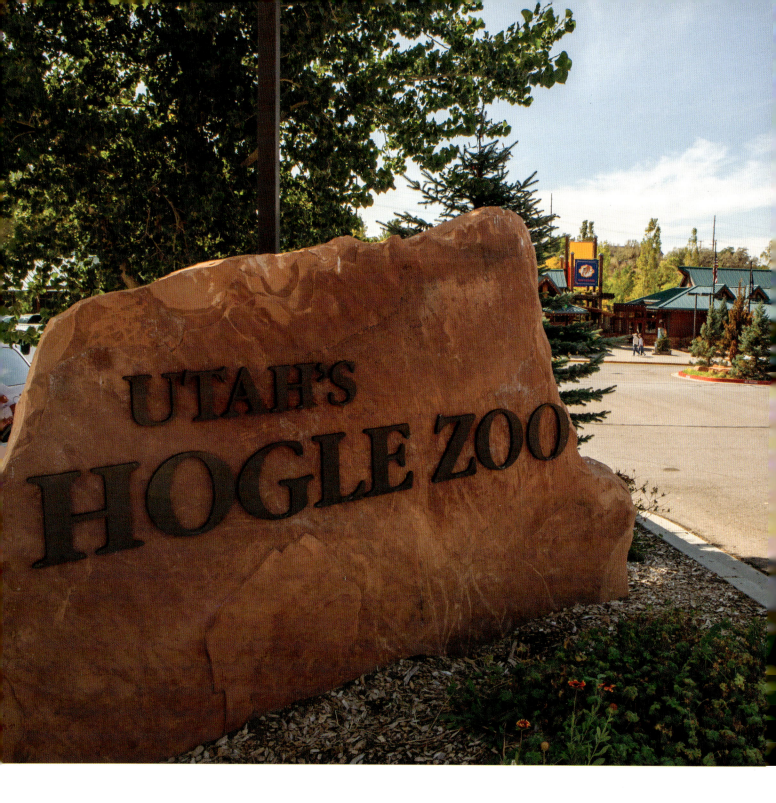

Hogle Zoo

Founded by the Hogle family in 1931, Hogel Zoo is one of Utah's most visited attractions. Positioned at the mouth of Emigration Canyon on 42 acres of natural terrain, with tree-lined pathways and more than 800 animals, it isn't hard to see why people are fascinated by this extraordinary destination.

African Elephant *(top)*

With large ears shaped like the continent of Africa, Hogle Zoo proudly hosts several African elephants. The popular Elephant Encounter exhibit brings a bit of the Serengeti to visitors who enjoy watching the dynamics of white rhinos and elephants in four outdoor habitats and the African Lodge.

Baringo Giraffe *(bottom)*

With an average height of 17 feet and a weight of 3,000 pounds, a male Baringo giraffe can eat up to 75 pounds of food each day! These amazing animals are just one of the countless reasons why more than 1,000,000 people have visited Salt Lake City's exceptional Hogle Zoo.

Zoo Lights *(top and bottom)*

Over 250 light displays make Hogle Zoo a dazzling holiday destination. With magical moving parts set to festive music, this glittering spectacle is like nothing else in the city. A full-range sound system makes Zoo Lights positively electrifying as Santa, live reindeer, and warm treats brighten up winter nights.

Rocky Shores *(opposite)*

Hogle Zoo's extensive multi-animal habitat, Rocky Shores, marked the much-anticipated return of polar bears to Utah. With the coolest seals, sea lions, river otters, and polar and grizzly bears around, Rocky Shores allows visitors to get up close and personal through underwater viewing stations and interactive technology.

EnergySolutions Arena

Home of the Utah Jazz, in addition to a myriad of other sporting and special events, EnergySolutions Arena is "the largest and most high-tech arena within a five state radius." Ice shows, live concerts, and the Ringling Brothers Circus all regularly come to this 22,000-seat Utah showpiece.

Olympic Oval *(top)*

Currently boasting the fastest ice in the world, which has contributed to more world records than any other venue, this superior indoor speed-skating oval was built for the 2002 Winter Olympic Games. Located in Kearns, just 14 miles southwest of Salt Lake City, The Oval is now open to the public.

Speed Skating *(bottom)*

The only private facility of its kind in the world, this Olympic training venue continues to host international athletes as they prepare for upcoming events, in addition to offering public skating, rentals, and special events. The Oval is open daily throughout most of the year, but is closed on December 25th.

Salt Lake City Marathon *(opposite)*

Beginning at the Olympic Legacy Bridge on the U of U campus, and finishing at Olympic Legacy Plaza at The Gateway downtown, the Salt Lake City Marathon has been a national favorite since 2004. In subsequent years, both a bike race and a half-marathon were enthusiastically added.

Salt Lake Bees *(above)*

At home in Salt Lake City's Spring Mobile Ballpark, this local minor league baseball team plays in the AAA Pacific Coast League. As the top affiliate of Major League Baseball's Los Angeles Angels of Anaheim, the Salt Lake Bees retain particularly loyal fans, which have cheered them on since 1994.

Wheeler Historic Farm Animals *(above)*

One of the few remaining 19th-century farms in the Valley, the 1898 Wheeler Historic Farm sits on 75 acres of fertile land in Murray, Utah. Visitors can milk a cow, ride in a wagon, watch a duck in the pond, or pet a new baby animal in the springtime.

Wheeler Historic Farm *(opposite)*

Established by Henry J. Wheeler at the age of 20, along with his new, hard-working wife, Sariah Pixton, the Wheeler farm became a model of beauty and industry. Purchased by Salt Lake County in 1969, it's now operated by Salt Lake County Parks and Recreation and offers free daily activities.

Great Salt Lake Sunrise *(top)*

The Great Salt Lake is the largest saltwater lake in the Western Hemisphere. Covering 1,700 square miles in an average year, this brackish lake's area fluctuates significantly, largely due to its shallow depth. Similar to the ocean, striking sunrises are commonplace here, yet this lake is far saltier than the sea.

America's Dead Sea *(bottom)*

The chief remnant of ancient Lake Bonneville, a prehistoric body of water that covered much of what is now Western Utah, the Great Salt Lake's lone outlet is evaporation. In addition to floating swimmers with ease, it provides habitat for brine shrimp and birds, and is sometimes called "America's Dead Sea."

Bingham Canyon Mine *(top)*

Twenty-five miles from downtown, this mine has been extracting essential elements from the Oquirrh Mountains since 1906. Operated by Kennecott Utah Copper Corporation and owned by Rio Tinto Corp., it is the deepest open-pit mining operation in the world. Tours are available from April through October.

Snowbird *(bottom)*

Just east of Salt Lake City, minutes up Little Cottonwood Canyon, an unincorporated area known as Snowbird lies cradled among the Wasatch Mountains. This scenic wonderland is most recognized for the Snowbird Ski and Summer Resort that offers legendary skiing, snowboarding, and summer activities.

Big Cottonwood Canyon *(above)*

Spectacular landscapes in Big Cottonwood Canyon were created as rivers carved their way through the steep, rugged terrain. Twelve miles from the city, this stunning ravine features superb scenery and recreational opportunities. In roughly twenty minutes, city residents can enjoy the Solitude or Brighton Ski Areas with ease.

Albion Basin in Alta *(opposite)*

With a trailhead elevation of 9,000 feet, Albion Basin bikers and hikers often feel shortness of breath. Amid stunning wildflowers at Cecret Lake, campers call the landscape "simply breathtaking," as do skiers at the fabulous Alta Ski Area. So clearly, though just minutes above the city, Albion Basin leaves visitors breathless!

Park City (top)

About thirty miles southeast of Salt Lake City, a world-famous winter sports community awaits. This popular tourist destination is home to three major ski resorts: Park City Mountain Resort, Deer Valley Resort, and Canyons Resort, as well as home to a large factory outlet mall and a popular symphony series.

Main Street (bottom)

Historic Main Street in Park City features luxurious boutiques, art galleries, and high-end gift shops, in addition to some of Utah's finest dining establishments and pubs. Festivals, concerts, and street markets are common along this well-traveled thoroughfare where celebrities frequently mingle with the locals.

Sundance Film Festival *(above)*

All eyes are on Park City as America's largest independent film fête, the Sundance Film Festival, gets underway. Once a thriving mining settlement, this quaint community still thrives as a retreat for the rich and famous—attracting stars and movie buffs worldwide for this highly anticipated annual event.

Hot Air Balloon Festival *(pages 120 – 121)*

Just 15 miles from downtown, a colorful wave of hot air balloons launches into an August morning sky at the annual Hot Air Balloon Festival in Sandy. Snow cones, pizza, and burgers abound—in addition to live musical entertainment. The magic heightens at dusk as the ever-popular "Balloon Glow" begins.

Snowbird Torchlight Parade

Snowbird's festive holiday events conclude each year on December 31st with a New Year's Eve Torchlight Parade and fireworks show. At this stunning annual event, literally hundreds of skiers carry twin-tipped bamboo torches down Snowbird Mountain, inspiring a steady stream of light and a truly astounding spectacle.

Airborne in Park City

Skiers come from all over the world to "catch air" above the legendary Utah powder. This natural high is continually repeated each winter at the Park City Mountain Resort where jumps and moguls are plentiful. Three versatile terrain parks, designed for all ages and abilities, augment this top-notch resort.

Deer Valley Summer

An outdoor adventurer's paradise, Deer Valley is extraordinary by nature—even after the snow melts. Hikers, explorers, and mountain bikers can weave from aspen forests to grassy meadows, surrounded only by clean mountain air. Exceptional dining, outdoor concerts, and first-class accommodations make this an ideal getaway.

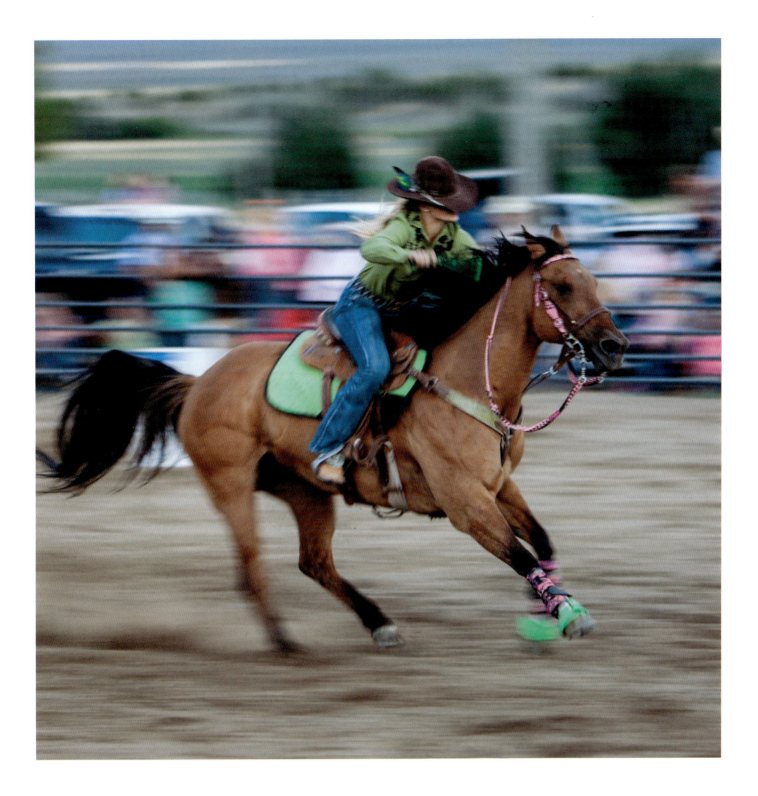

Rodeo Fun

From the celebrated Days of '47 Rodeo, to the fiery local stampedes, roping and racing abound for rodeo enthusiasts in and around Salt Lake City during the summer months. Spine-cracking bronco rides and bone-crushing bullfights lure thousands of eager spectators to grand stands all across the Intermountain West each year.

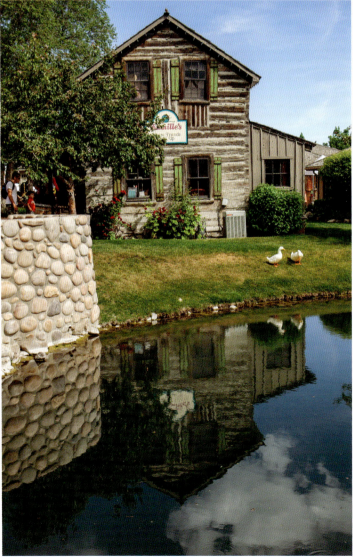

Gardner Village Farmers' Market *(above)*

Established in 1853, Gardner Village is home to a variety of charming shops, as well as a popular farmer's market. It was Archibald Gardner, a pioneer businessman and millwright, who helped establish the community of West Jordan, near Salt Lake City, where Gardner's life is memorialized at "Archibald's Restaurant."

Gardner Village *(left)*

Kamille's yarn shop is just one of 25 boutiques and restaurants nestled within the homes, cabins, and buildings where a bustling gristmill once stood. Vintage architecture and a bridge-covered pond help provide the quaint atmosphere for which this homegrown event haven is still known and cherished today.

La Caille Restaurant in Sandy *(opposite)*

La Caille's elegant setting where deer, rabbits, swans, and peacocks openly roam, provides an exquisite natural backdrop for the antique-lined dining areas where dinner and Sunday Brunch are presented—and where special events and weddings are sumptuously catered. Dining here is a pleasure.

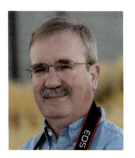

Bill Crnkovich

Bill Crnkovich is a native of Wisconsin and has lived in Connecticut and Virginia. Since 1994, he and his family have resided in South Jordan, Utah. His passion for the outdoors frequently takes him to the mountains and deserts: from the Grand Tetons to southern Utah's red rock country. Bill's background as a Mechanical Engineer is reflected in his attention to detail. He established Best of the West Photography in 2000 to showcase his magnificent western landscapes. His award-winning pictures grace many calendars and publications. To see more of Bill's work, visit www.BestWestPhoto.com.

DeAnne Flynn

DeAnne Flynn has lived in seven U.S. states, but proudly calls Utah home. A high honor graduate of Brigham Young University, DeAnne has worked as a news anchor/reporter, a corporate marketing director and spokesperson, a freelance script and copywriter, and as a touring national presenter with Time Out for Women. She discovered her passion for writing books by authoring The Time-Starved Family (2009) and The Mother's Mite (2011) while living in a shady community near Salt Lake City with her husband, seven children, beloved morky, and two vociferous parakeets. She gladly welcomes visitors at www.deanneflynn.com.